# Musk Oxen

## SANDRA MARKLE

LERNER PUBLICATIONS COMPANY / MINNEAPOLIS

# The Animal World
## Is Full of
# PREY.

Prey are the animals that predators eat. Predators must find, catch, kill, and eat other animals in order to survive. But prey animals aren't always easy to catch or kill. Some have eyes on the sides of their heads to let them see predators coming from all directions. Some are colored to blend in and hide. Some prey are built to run, leap, fly, or swim fast to get away. And still others sting, bite, or use chemicals to keep predators away.

In the Arctic, the northernmost area of the world, one kind of prey is especially well equipped to survive both the harsh environment and fierce predators. *That animal is the musk ox.*

At midnight in May, it's still light in the very far north of Canada. To the musk oxen living there, more light means more time to eat. Musk oxen are about 5 feet (1.5 meters) tall at the shoulder hump. With hair hanging to their knees, they look like small, shaggy buffalo. At this time of the year, the animals are shedding clumps of fine hair, their winter undercoat.

Every step or two, each musk ox grabs a mouthful of the tough, grasslike sedges that grow in the far north. But even as they eat, the animals' big eyes, set high on their heads, look out for predators.

Suddenly, the herd's lead cow (female musk ox) lifts her head. Her calf lifts his head too, sensing his mother's nervousness. The lead cow snorts and starts running.

Although the herd has spread out to graze, the other musk oxen immediately race after the cow. Hooves thud like drumbeats on the frozen ground, as their long hair flies like billowing skirts behind the oxen's short legs. Musk oxen can run fast. But the danger the lead cow spotted—a pack of arctic wolves—is catching up.

The herd continues running until they reach the top of a gentle slope. Then the adults turn to face the wolves. But the wolves are no longer chasing the whole herd. They've focused on just one animal—the lead cow's calf. Hunting as a team is the only way the wolves can take on such big prey. Even then, the wolf pack's best chance of making a kill is to attack one of the smaller or weaker and slower members of the herd.

Bellowing, the lead cow swings around and charges to defend her young. Even though they are big, musk oxen are agile and quick. The adults are also armed with big, sharp horns.

*The herd's two young bulls (males) join in the attack.* The wolves run away rather than risk being injured. This time, the musk oxen's size and horns have won out over the predators' speed and sharp teeth.

The danger passed, the herd soon returns to grazing its way across the tundra, the treeless plains of the far north. Sedges are the main plants growing there. To get enough nutrition, musk oxen need to eat a lot of plant matter every day.

The lead cow's calf trails after his mother. He begins to bleat plaintively to be fed. When his mother finally stands still for him, he noses under the tent of his mother's shaggy coat, finds a teat, and suckles.

A few days later, the small herd joins another larger herd. The two groups of musk oxen are familiar with one another and have traveled together before. A larger group is safer for everyone, especially the calves. Food is plentiful because this is the growing season for the tundra plants. There are enough plants for a large number of musk oxen to graze close together.

Besides eating, the musk oxen spend a lot of time lying around digesting what they've eaten. Like cows, musk oxen chew their cud, food swallowed earlier and stored in their stomach until they bring it up to chew again. The second chewing helps break down the tough sedges to make them easier to digest.

After a brief summer, the days grow shorter, and the weather gets colder. It's fall on the tundra—the season when the musk ox cows are ready to mate. They signal their readiness with a strong scent in their urine, which clings to their hair. When a musk ox bull smells this scent, his behavior changes dramatically.

The biggest bull immediately tries to take control of the cows. He guards them and waits for his chance to mate. But soon a lone male arrives to fight the big bull for the females.

When the two bulls face off, the defender lowers his head. This is a silent threat. It presents the best possible view of his horns. Both rivals snort and paw the ground. Next, the newcomer backs off nearly 50 feet (15 meters), and the two bulls face off again. Each has his eyes locked on the other's face. Then the new bull gives his final challenge. He slowly waggles his head to display all parts of his horns to the defending bull.

The cows and calves watch intently as the challenger runs toward the defender. His hair whips around his legs as he flies across the ground at nearly 25 miles (40 kilometers) per hour. The rivals maintain eye contact as the distance between them closes. Then the defender shifts his position, readying himself for the impact.

*Crack! With a sound as loud as a rifle shot,* the rivals crash their helmetlike horns together. At the moment of impact, the new bull pushes. He tries to make the defender turn and expose his side to attack. If that happens, he would gore his rival in the belly. But this time, the defender is ready. He moves forward just as he is hit and is able to begin to turn the other bull. The battle continues this way for almost an hour. The two stand snorting, with their foreheads and long noses pressed together.

*Quickly, the new bull breaks free.* Then he turns and charges again. He still doesn't defeat the big bull. Finally, the new bull leaves. The defender has won the right to mate. Even so, each cow decides if she will mate or not. She may just walk away when the male approaches. Or the male may have to defend his right to mate against another rival.

The competition only lasts a short time, though, because each female is ready to mate for only a day or two. Within a couple of weeks, the musk oxen are back to eating. This is especially important for the bulls. They don't eat much during the mating period. To prepare for winter, they need to build up a layer of stored fat and grow an undercoat.

*The days grow shorter, and snow begins to pile up on the ground.* The musk oxen split up into small herds again. There are herds of bachelor males and herds of cows with calves, yearlings, and a few young adult males. These herds migrate (travel) to their winter ranges. The trip is usually short—less than 50 miles (80 kilometers). But it usually takes them to a high, barren area where strong winds keep the snow from piling up too high. The musk oxen are able to crush through the icy crust with their hooves. Then they dig a hole, called a feeding crater, in the snow to reach the frozen sedges buried underneath.

The fierce winter weather is hard on the young musk oxen. Their bodies are smaller and have less stored fat to protect them from the cold.

When cold winds blow, the adults lie down to keep as much of their bodies as they can away from the sharp wind. The bodies of the adult oxen provide a little shelter from the full blast of the wind. So the calves lie down close together beside one of the biggest cows.

During fierce blizzards, snow piles up on the musk oxen. The snow doesn't melt on them. This is because their downy undercoat traps body heat next to their skin. The snow creates another layer of insulation from the cold wind.

The lead cow's calf survives the blizzard, but another calf doesn't. Its mother leaves it behind. She walks away through the drifting snow to follow the herd.

By February the days begin to get longer again. It's easier for the musk oxen to find food, but it's also easier for the wolves to track the herd. One day the musk oxen spot a pack of wolves traveling along a ridge. The adult oxen watch the hunters and become more and more nervous.

Snorting, one of the young bulls turns his back on the wolves and runs away. Immediately, the others run after him.

The lead cow's calf sticks close to his mother's heels. But a smaller calf is soon left behind. It bleats plaintively. But the herd keeps running, and the small calf falls even farther behind.

Loping along after the musk oxen, the wolf pack spots the trailing calf. The team of hunters immediately splits up. Some chase after the adults to keep them running. Two wolves home in on the calf, cutting it off from the herd.

*The herd stops abruptly and moves into its defensive position.*
The oxen stand shoulder to shoulder facing the wolves. The calves are pressed together in the middle of this living fortress. The wolves circle the snorting, pawing musk oxen. Snarling and snapping their jaws, one wolf and then another wolf charges the herd. They retreat just in time to avoid being gored by the musk oxen's sharp horns. These charges are enough to keep the herd together.

Without any adults to come to its rescue, the calf is easy prey. One wolf leaps on it, bringing it crashing to the ground. Then the other wolf joins in the attack and bites the calf's throat to make the kill. The rest of the pack immediately abandons the attack on the musk oxen herd. Each wolf rushes to grab a share of the fresh meat. While the wolves eat, the rest of the musk oxen run away.

Three years pass as the musk oxen migrate between winter and summer grazing ranges. They are constantly alert for predators. During this time, the young calf becomes a yearling and then a young adult bull. When he's about three years old, he leaves his mother's herd and joins a group of other bulls. Some of the bulls are his age, and some are older.

While he's getting bigger and his horns are growing, he plays at battling the other bulls. This way he develops his endurance and his skills.

One summer, while he's grazing alongside a herd of cows and their calves, two wolves attack. The other members of the herd immediately swivel away from the danger and thunder away. But the young bull turns and charges at the hunters. Weighing nearly 1,000 pounds (454 kilograms), he's not easy prey. The wolf just behind the bull stops short. Snorting, the bull lowers his head and waggles it to show off his horns. The wolves snarl but don't attack. The standoff is brief, and the wolves leave.

The young bull has just proved he has the size and strength to control a herd of cows. Come fall, he'll battle for mating rights and win. And with the birth of his first calf, another generation of musk oxen will join the cycle of life, a constant struggle to survive between predators and prey.

# Looking Back

- Look back at the musk oxen on page 3. See how their woolly undercoats cling to their outercoats after they've been shed? Eventually, this hair blows off, falls off, or is combed out as the musk oxen pushes past low-growing shrubs.

- Flip through the book, paying special attention to what the musk oxen's home range looks like. What features of this terrain make standing close together a good defensive strategy for adult musk oxen?

- Look closely at page 34 to check out the musk oxen's feet. Their foot structure and their broad, sharp-edged hooves help them be sure-footed on uneven rocks, snow, and icy ground.

- Compare the calves on pages 11 and 37 to the adult musk oxen. Besides getting bigger, in what ways will the youngsters change as they grow up?

# Glossary

BULL: a male musk ox

CALF: a baby musk ox

COW: a female musk ox

HERD: a group of musk oxen traveling together

HOOF: a hard covering on an animal's foot for protection when walking. Musk oxen have very broad hooves to help them walk in snow. The hoof also has a sharp edge to prevent the animal from slipping on hard-packed snow and ice.

HORNS: a hard, bony structure on the head that is used for defense. Musk ox horns are made of keratin, much like human fingernails. A musk ox bull's horns form a helmetlike plate across its forehead.

PREDATOR: an animal that hunts and eats other animals in order to survive

PREY: an animal that a predator catches to eat

STOMACH: the organ in the body where food is broken down

TUNDRA: the nearly flat, treeless plain in the Arctic region of North America, Europe, and Asia

# More Information

## Books

Love, Ann, Jane Drake, and Jocelyn Bouchard. *The Kids Book of the Far North.* Toronto: Kids Can Press, 2000. This book discusses the Arctic region and the plants, animals, and people who live there.

Markle, Sandra. *Wolves.* Minneapolis: Lerner Publications Company, 2004. Learn about one of the musk oxen's main predators.

Rau, Margaret. *Musk Oxen: Bearded Ones of the Arctic.* New York: HarperCollins, 1976. This book is an introduction to the physical features of musk oxen and describes how the animal survives.

## Video

*Alaska's Arctic Wildlife.* Danbury, CT: WonderVisions, 1997. Enjoy the chance to virtually visit this vast wilderness area and witness wildlife interacting, including battling male musk oxen.

## Websites

Muskox Farm
http://www.muskoxfarm.org/history.html
Visit a farm that raises musk oxen. Learn about wild populations, see babies, and check out an adult musk ox shedding qiviut.

Qiviut
http://www.qiviut.com
*Qiviut,* pronounced KIV-ee-ute, is the native word for the soft, downy hair of musk oxen. Learn how the hair is collected and used by native Alaskan people.

# Index

*With love, for Genista Friesen*

The author would like to thank the following people for sharing their expertise and enthusiasm: Dr. Perry Barboza, Associate Professor, Department of Biology and Wildlife, Institute of Arctic Biology, University of Alaska Fairbanks; Dr. Mads Forchhammer, Associate Professor, Department of Population Biology and Director of the Arctic Population Ecology Group, University of Copenhagen, Denmark; and William Hauer, Supervisor, Robert G. White Large Animal Research Station for the study of Musk Oxen, University of Alaska Fairbanks. The author would also like to express a special thank you to Skip Jeffery for his help and support during the creative process.

## Photo Acknowledgments

The images used in this book are used with permission of: © Erwin and Peggy Bauer/ Wildstock, pp. 1, 6, 23, 35; © NHPA/ B. C. Alexander, p. 3; © John Dunn/ National Geographic/ Getty Images, p. 4; © Jim Brandenburg/ National Geographic/ Getty Images, pp. 7, 9; © Naturbild/ Naturepl.com, p. 11; © Art Wolfe/ Art Wolfe Inc., p. 12; © YVA MOMATIUK/ JOHNEASTCOTT/ Minden Pictures, p. 13; © Eastcott Momatiuk/ Getty Images, p. 14; © Galen Rowell/ CORBIS, p. 15; © Tom and Pat Leeson, pp. 16, 17; © Michio Hoshino/ Minden Pictures, pp. 19, 34; © Tom Brakefield/ Photodisc Green/ Getty Images, p. 20; © Wayne Lynch, p. 24; © Norbert Rosing/ National Geographic/ Getty Images, pp. 25, 26, 27, 30; © Jim Brandenburg/ Minden Pictures, pp. 28, 33, 36; © Tom Ulrich/ Oxford Scientific Films, p. 29; © Lynn M. Stone/ Naturepl.com, p. 31; © Chris Schenk/ Foto Natura/ Minden Pictures, p. 37. Front Cover: © Joseph Van Os/ The Image Bank/ Getty Images.

Lerner Publications Company
A division of Lerner Publishing Group
241 First Avenue North
Minneapolis, MN 55401

Website address: www.lernerbooks.com

Library of Congress Cataloging-in-Publication Data

Markle, Sandra.
    Musk oxen / by Sandra Markle.
      p.    cm. — (Animal prey)
    Includes bibliographical references and index.
    ISBN-13: 978—0—8225—6064—7 (lib. bdg. : alk. paper)
    ISBN-10: 0—8225—6064—X (lib. bdg. : alk. paper)
    1. Muskox—Juvenile literature. I. Title.
QL737.U53M37 2007
599.64'78—dc22                          599.64'78—dc22

Manufactured in the United States of America
1 2 3 4 5 6 — DP — 12 11 10 09 08 07